MADE IN FRANCE

Cross-Stitch
Samplers

Marjorie Massey

MADE IN FRANCE

Cross-Stitch
Samplers

Photography by Frédéric Lucano
Styling by Sonia Lucano

Charts by Christine Toufflet

MURDOCH BOOKS

To our great delight, Marjorie Massey has thrown open the doors of her workshop to us. This insatiable antique-lover has gleaned many pieces of embroidery over the years, which she uses as inspiration in designing her own samplers, alphabets and small pictures imbued with charm and poetry. She preciously guards them and, after rummaging through her cupboards, rifling through her drawers and up-ending her travel chests, she invites us to discover in these pages some of her loveliest patterns, alternately in red or blue according to the fancy of the day. Sometimes there is no J or W in the alphabets, as in samplers of former times… sometimes an antique frieze speaks to her and she reassembles, remodels and adapts it… sometimes she is inspired by antique motifs and she reworks, colours and transforms them. Each design is unique, personal and always timeless, each one enchants anew with its detail, composition and balance. Surrender to their charm and embroider with abandon…

ABCDF G
HIJKL♥M

nopqrs 12345
67 0
8 0 tuvwxyz

ALPHABETS (pattern sheet I)

Design size: 184 x 184 stitches
Dimensions according to fabric weave:
40-count fabric: 23 x 23 cm
36-count fabric: 26 x 26 cm
30-count fabric: 31 x 31 cm
Stitches used: cross-stitch and backstitch
Skeins of DMC Mouliné stranded cotton nos 791, 792 and 3839

Begin the design in the centre. Leave a margin of at least 6 cm all around the embroidery.
Work the backstitch using a thread that matches the motif you are embroidering. Use the numbers on pattern sheet I to personalise your embroidery. You can also embroider this design in red. In that case, replace the DMC Mouliné no. 791 with 816, 792 with 304 and 3839 with 309.

MOTIF SAMPLERS (charts pages 60-61)

Design size: 56 x 124 stitches
Dimensions according to fabric weave:
40-count fabric: 8 x 15 cm
36-count fabric: 9 x 17 cm
30-count fabric: 11 x 22 cm
Stitch used: cross-stitch
Skeins of DMC Mouliné stranded cotton nos 791, 792 and 3839

Begin the design in the centre. Leave a margin of at least 6 cm all around the embroidery.
You can also embroider this design in red. In that case, replace DMC Mouliné no. 791 with 816, 792 with 304 and 3839 with 309.

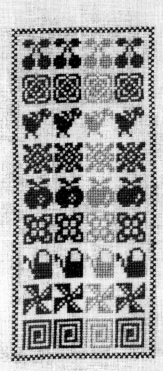

· DMC · NEEDLEWORK FABRICS · DMC · TOILES A BRODER · DMC · NEEDLEWORK FABRICS · DM

SMALL SAMPLER (chart page 62)

Design size: 130 x 81 stitches
Dimensions according to fabric weave:
40-count fabric: 17 x 10 cm
36-count fabric: 20 x 12 cm
30-count fabric: 23 x 14 cm
Stitch used: cross-stitch
Skein of DMC Mouliné stranded cotton no. 498

Begin the design in the centre. Leave a margin of at least 6 cm all around the embroidery.

AMITIÉ ("FRIENDSHIP") (chart page 63)

Design size: 137 x 85 stitches
Dimensions according to fabric weave:
40-count fabric: 17 x 11 cm
36-count fabric: 20 x 13 cm
30-count fabric: 23 x 15 cm
Stitch used: cross-stitch
Skein of DMC Mouliné stranded cotton no. 498

Begin the design in the centre. Leave a margin of at least 6 cm all around the embroidery.

BIENVENUE ET BON SÉJOUR ("WELCOME AND ENJOY YOUR STAY") (chart pages 64-65)

Design size: 128 x 81 stitches
Dimensions according to fabric weave:
40-count fabric: 16 x 11 cm
36-count fabric: 18 x 13 cm
30-count fabric: 21 x 15 cm
Stitches used: cross-stitch and backstitch
Skeins of DMC Mouliné stranded cotton nos 304 and 309

Begin the design in the centre. Leave a margin of at least 6 cm all around the embroidery.
Work the backstitch using a thread that matches the embroidered motif.

ROUGE CERISE ("CHERRY RED") (chart pages 66-67)

Design size: 143 x 87 stitches
Dimensions according to fabric weave:
40-count fabric: 18 x 11 cm
36-count fabric: 21 x 13 cm
30-count fabric: 24 x 15 cm
Stitch used: cross-stitch
Skein of DMC Mouliné stranded cotton no. 498

Begin the design in the centre. Leave a margin of at least 6 cm all around the embroidery.

BIENVENUE ET BON SÉJOUR (chart pages 64–65)

ROMANTIC (pattern sheet II)

Design size: 383 x 280 stitches
Dimensions according to fabric weave:
40-count fabric: 48 x 35 cm
36-count fabric: 55 x 40 cm
30-count fabric: 64 x 47 cm
Stitch used: cross-stitch
Skeins of DMC Mouliné stranded cotton no. 498

Begin the design in the centre. Leave a margin of at least 6 cm all around the embroidery.
Use numbers from pattern sheet II to personalise your embroidery.

Two roosters (chart pages 68-69)

Design size: 133 x 133 stitches
Dimensions according to fabric weave:
40-count fabric: 17 x 17 cm
36-count fabric: 19 x 19 cm
30-count fabric: 22 x 22 cm
Stitch used: cross-stitch
Skeins of DMC Mouliné stranded cotton no. 792

Begin the design in the centre. Leave a margin of at least 6 cm all around the embroidery.

TWO REINDEER (chart page 70)

Design size: 99 x 90 stitches
Dimensions according to fabric weave:
40-count fabric: 13 x 12 cm
36-count fabric: 14 x 13 cm
30-count fabric: 16 x 15 cm
Stitches used: cross-stitch and backstitch
Skeins of DMC Mouliné stranded cotton no. 498

Begin the design in the centre. Leave a margin of at least 6 cm all around the embroidery.
In this motif the background is embroidered, leaving the non-embroidered areas to reveal the design.
Use the numbers to personalise your embroidery: the larger ones for either end and the smaller numbers for the two in the middle.

BIENVENUE ("WELCOME") (pattern sheet I)

Design size: 143 x 163 stitches
Dimensions according to fabric weave:
40-count fabric: 18 x 20 cm
36-count fabric: 21 x 23 cm
30-count fabric: 24 x 27 cm
Stitch used: cross-stitch
Skeins of DMC Mouliné stranded cotton no. 498

Begin the design in the centre. Leave a margin of at least 6 cm all around the embroidery.
Use the extra numbers from pattern sheet I to personalise your embroidery.

HOUSE WITH HEART (chart page 72)

Design size: 89 x 89 stitches
Dimensions according to fabric weave:
40-count fabric: 11 x 11 cm
36-count fabric: 13 x 13 cm
30-count fabric: 15 x 15 cm
Stitch used: cross-stitch
Skeins of DMC Mouliné stranded cotton no. 304

Begin the design in the centre. Leave a margin of at least 6 cm all around the embroidery.
Use the extra numbers and appropriate letters from the alphabet on page 72 to personalise
your embroidery.

FOLK ALPHABET (chart page 73)

Design size: 87 x 87 stitches
Dimensions according to fabric weave:
40-count fabric: 11 x 11 cm
36-count fabric: 13 x 13 cm
30-count fabric: 15 x 15 cm
Stitch used: cross-stitch
Skeins of DMC Mouliné stranded cotton no. 304

Begin the design in the centre. Leave a margin of at least 6 cm all around the embroidery.
Use the extra numbers from page 73 to personalise your embroidery.

LITTLE DONKEY (pattern sheet V)

Design size: 203 x 142 stitches
Dimensions according to fabric weave:
40-count fabric: 25 x 18 cm
36-count fabric: 29 x 20 cm
30-count fabric: 34 x 24 cm
Stitch used: cross-stitch
Skeins of DMC Mouliné stranded cotton nos 816 and 309

Begin the design in the centre. Leave a margin of at least 6 cm all around the embroidery.
For the medium red, use one strand of Mouliné dark red cotton no. 816 and one strand of Mouliné light red no. 309 together. That way, you'll obtain a new and more subtle colour.

ALL HEART (charts pages 74 to 77)

Instructions for making one heart

Design size: 81 x 75 stitches
Dimensions according to fabric weave:
40-count fabric: 10 x 9.5 cm
36-count fabric: 12 x 11 cm
30-count fabric: 14 x 12.5 cm
Stitches used: cross-stitch and backstitch
Skeins of DMC Mouliné stranded cotton no. 792

Begin the design in the centre. Leave a margin of at least 8 cm all around the embroidery.
The outlines of the hearts are sewn in backstitch. Use 1 strand for 40-count fabrics and 2 strands for fabrics with 6 or 7 stitches/cm.

HEART WITH FOX (chart page 78)

33

HEART WITH BIRDS (chart page 78)

Design size: 71 x 60 stitches
Dimensions according to fabric weave:
40-count fabric: 9 x 8 cm
36-count fabric: 10 x 9 cm
30-count fabric: 11.5 x 10 cm
Stitches used: cross-stitch and backstitch
Skeins of DMC Mouliné stranded cotton no. 791

Begin the design in the centre. Leave a margin of at least 6 cm all around the embroidery.

HEART WITH FOX (chart page 78)

Design size: 69 x 61 stitches
Dimensions according to fabric weave:
40-count fabric: 9 x 8 cm
36-count fabric: 10 x 9 cm
30-count fabric: 11.5 x 10 cm
Stitches used: cross-stitch and backstitch
Skeins of DMC Mouliné stranded cotton no. 791

Begin the design in the centre. Leave a margin of at least 6 cm all around the embroidery.

BONJOUR (chart page 79)

Design size: 99 x 141 stitches
Dimensions according to fabric weave:
40-count fabric: 13 x 18 cm
36-count fabric: 14 x 20 cm
30-count fabric: 16.5 x 23.5 cm
Stitches used: cross-stitch
Skeins of DMC Mouliné stranded cotton nos 791, 792 and 3839

Begin the design in the centre. Leave a margin of at least 6 cm all around the embroidery.

À CHAQUE JOUR SUFFIT SA PEINE ("SUFFICIENT UNTO THE DAY IS THE EVIL THEREOF") (chart pages 80-81)

Design size: 136 x 107 stitches
Dimensions according to fabric weave:
40-count fabric: 17 x 13 cm
36-count fabric: 19.5 x 15 cm
30-count fabric: 22.5 x 18 cm
Stitches used: cross-stitch and backstitch
Skeins of DMC Mouliné stranded cotton nos 792, 824 or 825

Begin the design in the centre. Leave a margin of at least 6 cm all around the embroidery.

HOUSE WITH CATS (chart pages 82-83)

Design size: 81 x 121 stitches
Dimensions according to fabric weave:
40-count fabric: 10 x 16 cm
36-count fabric: 12 x 18 cm
30-count fabric: 14 x 20 cm
Stitch used: cross-stitch
Skeins of DMC Mouliné stranded cotton no. 304

Begin the design in the centre. Leave a margin of at least 6 cm all around the embroidery.
Use the extra numbers from page 83 to personalise your embroidery.

SAMPLER WITH CATS (chart pages 84-85)

Design size: 81 x 185 stitches
Dimensions according to fabric weave:
40-count fabric: 10 x 23 cm
36-count fabric: 12 x 27 cm
30-count fabric: 14 x 31 cm
Stitch used: cross-stitch
Skeins of DMC Mouliné stranded cotton no. 304

Begin the design in the centre. Leave a margin of at least 6 cm all around the embroidery.

MADELEINE (pattern sheet IV)

Design size: 299 x 231 stitches
Dimensions according to fabric weave:
40-count fabric: 38 x 29 cm
36-count fabric: 43 x 33 cm
30-count fabric: 50 x 39 cm
Stitches used: cross-stitch and backstitch
Skeins of DMC Mouliné stranded cotton no. 498

Begin the design in the centre. Leave a margin of at least 6 cm all around the embroidery.

BLACKBERRY JAM (pattern sheet V)

FRUIT TILES (chart pages 86-87)

Design size: 149 x 149 stitches
Dimensions according to fabric weave:
40-count fabric: 19 x 19 cm
36-count fabric: 21 x 21 cm
30-count fabric: 25 x 25 cm
Stitches used: cross-stitch
Skeins of DMC Mouliné stranded cotton nos 791, 792 and 3839

Begin the design in the centre. Leave a margin of at least 6 cm all around the embroidery. You can also embroider this pattern in red. In that case, replace DMC Mouliné no. 791 with 150, 792 with 816 and 3839 with 309.

BLACKBERRY JAM (pattern sheet V)

Design size: 149 x 149 stitches
Dimensions according to fabric weave:
40-count fabric: 19 x 19 cm
36-count fabric: 21 x 21 cm
30-count fabric: 25 x 25 cm
Stitches used: cross-stitch and backstitch
Skeins of DMC Mouliné stranded cotton nos 791, 792 and 3839

Begin the design in the centre. Leave a margin of at least 6 cm all around the embroidery.

To embroider Strawberry jam (also on pattern sheet V), replace the blues with reds.
In that case, replace the DMC Mouliné no. 791 with 150, 792 with 816 and 3839 with 309, and swap the blackberry jam jar for the strawberry jam one.

PRETTY BUTTERFLY (chart page 71)

Design size: 116 x 81 stitches
Dimensions according to fabric weave:
40-count fabric: 17 x 12 cm
36-count fabric: 20 x 14 cm
30-count fabric: 21 x 15 cm
Stitch used: cross-stitch
Skeins of DMC Mouliné stranded cotton no. 791

Begin the design in the centre. Leave a margin of at least 6 cm all around the embroidery.

MONOGRAM WITH SQUARES (pattern sheet VI)

Design size: 215 x 149 stitches
Dimensions according to fabric weave:
40-count fabric: 27 x 19 cm
36-count fabric: 31 x 22 cm
40-count fabric: 36 x 25 cm
Stitch used: cross-stitch
Skeins of DMC Mouliné stranded cotton nos 823, 791 and 792

Begin the design in the centre. Leave a margin of at least 6 cm all around the embroidery.
Use the extra numbers and letters from pattern sheet VI to personalise your embroidery.

Fantasia (pattern sheet III)

Design size: 232 x 187 stitches
Dimensions according to fabric weave:
40-count fabric: 29 x 24 cm
36-count fabric: 33 x 27 cm
30-count fabric: 39 x 31 cm
Stitches used: cross-stitch and backstitch
Skeins of DMC Mouliné stranded cotton no. 498

Begin the design in the centre. Leave a margin of at least 6 cm all around the embroidery.
Use the extra numbers from pattern sheet III to personalise your embroidery.

SQUARE SAMPLER (chart pages 88-89)

Design size: 87 x 90 stitches
Dimensions according to fabric weave:
40-count fabric: 11 x 12 cm
36-count fabric: 12.5 x 13.5 cm
30-count fabric: 14.5 x 15.5 cm
Stitches used: cross-stitch, half cross-stitch and running stitch
Skeins of DMC Mouliné stranded cotton no. 498

Begin the design in the centre. Leave a margin of at least 6 cm all around the embroidery.
The horizontal lines represent the running stitches and the diagonal lines the half cross-stitches.
Use the extra letters from the alphabet on page 89 to personalise your embroidery.

ALPHABET WITH BUTTERFLIES (pattern sheets VII and VIII)

Design size: 261 x 209 stitches
Dimensions according to fabric weave:
40-count fabric: 33 x 26 cm
36-count fabric: 38 x 30 cm
30-count fabric: 44 x 35 cm
Stitches used: cross-stitch and backstitch
Skeins of DMC Mouliné stranded cotton no. 498

Begin the design in the centre. Leave a margin of at least 6 cm all around the embroidery.
Use the extra numbers and letters of the alphabet from sheet VIII to personalise your embroidery.

SUMMER SAMPLER (chart pages 90-91)

Design size: 64 x 194 stitches
Dimensions according to fabric weave:
40-count fabric: 8 x 24 cm
36-count fabric: 9 x 28 cm
30-count fabric: 11 x 33 cm
Stitches used: cross-stitch and backstitch
Skeins of DMC Mouliné stranded cotton no. 304 or 792

Begin the design in the centre. Leave a margin of at least 6 cm all around the embroidery.

MOTHER HEN (chart pages 92-93)

Design size: 64 x 230 stitches
Dimensions according to fabric weave:
40-count fabric: 8 x 29 cm
36-count fabric: 9 x 33 cm
30-count fabric: 11 x 38 cm
Stitches used: cross-stitch and backstitch
Skeins of DMC Mouliné stranded cotton no. 304 or 792

Begin the design in the centre. Leave a margin of at least 6 cm all around the embroidery.

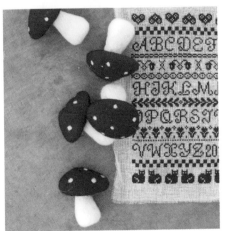

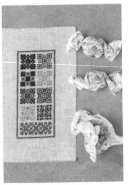

It's no secret to anyone: I adore monochrome embroideries in red and blue…

I mostly work with the DMC Mouliné stranded cottons. These cottons are colourfast, washable and don't shrink. They keep their magnificent colours over time, and even if they fade a little over the years, they retain their beauty and harmony.

The patterns in this new book are embroidered only in shades of red and blue. In the range of reds, my favourites are shade numbers 150, 304, 326, 498, 600 and 816… in the end almost all the reds except perhaps no. 347, which is much too orangey for my taste, but see it for yourself! As for the blues, my selection is a little narrower. The range is quite extensive but, I find, somewhat difficult to work with… I am very attracted to shade numbers 791, 792, 796, 3838 and 3839.

Most of the time, a simple change of colour gives the same pattern a completely different effect. For each embroidery I give colour-number recommendations, but please don't let that stop you from changing shades or even whole ranges. Also, when you are looking for a particular nuance in a set of shades, do as I do and combine two numbers in order to obtain the desired hue… The new "colour" is often incredibly soft and subtle.

I don't give any indications for kind of fabric or colour. Open your drawers, visit the haberdashery stores and let yourself be open to temptation. Keep in mind, however, the following basic rules, which will help you avoid less attractive results.

In general, 25-count (or 5 stitches/cm) fabrics are embroidered using 2 strands of DMC Mouliné cotton over 2 warp and weave threads. 36-count (or 7 stitches/cm) linen or even-weave fabrics are embroidered using 1 or 2 strands of DMC Mouliné cotton over 2 warp and weave threads, depending on how raised and thick you want the stitches to be. Sew a small sample by embroidering a few lines of stitches to gauge the effect. As for 40-count (or 8 stitches/cm) fabrics, these are usually embroidered using 1 strand DMC Mouliné stranded cotton over 1 thread of fabric.

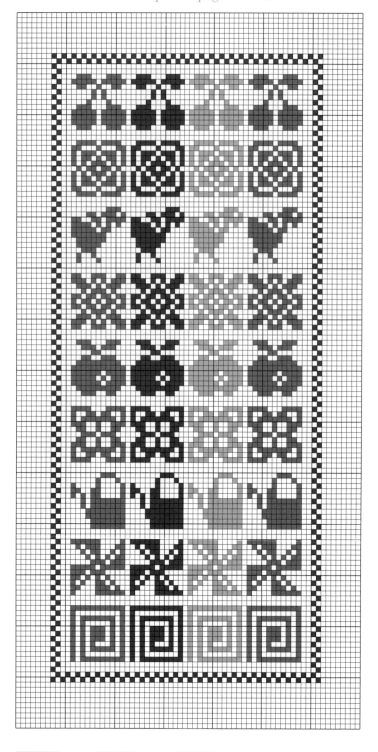

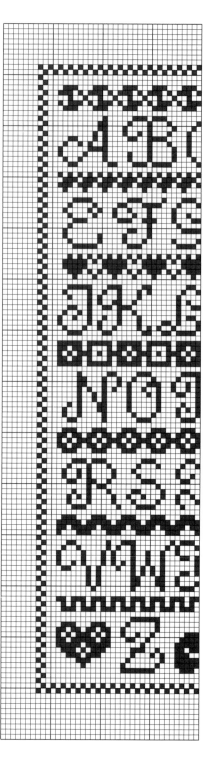

791   792   3839

304   309

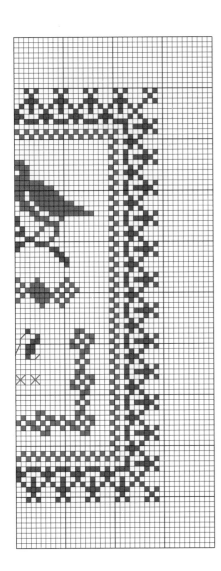

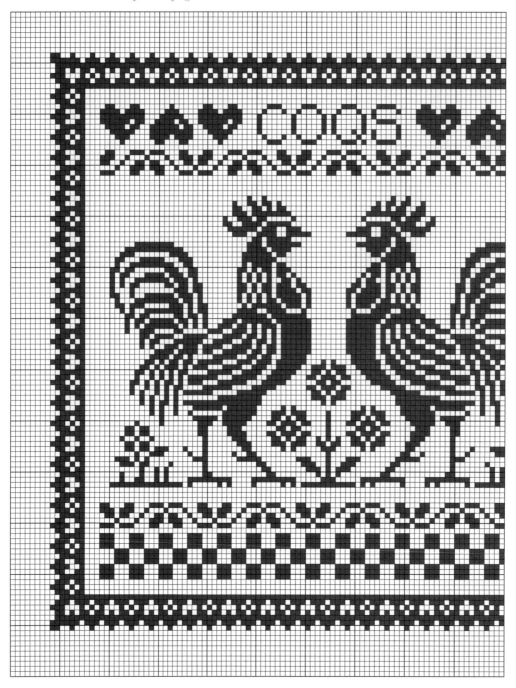

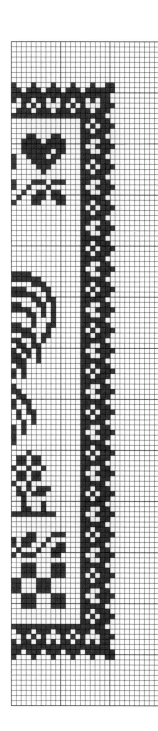

Feel free to change the look of this design by
embroidering it in red, for example.

(1)

(2)

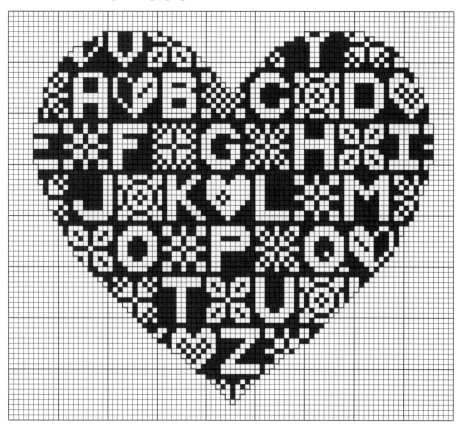

Feel free to change the look of these hearts by embroidering them in red, for example.

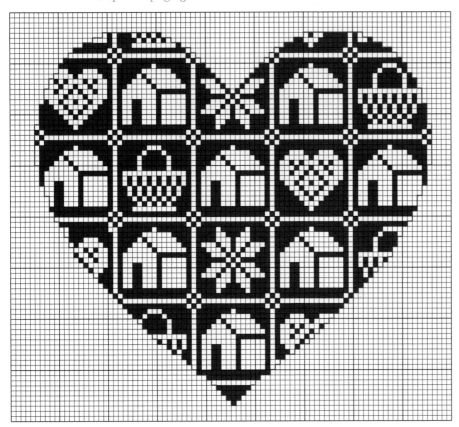

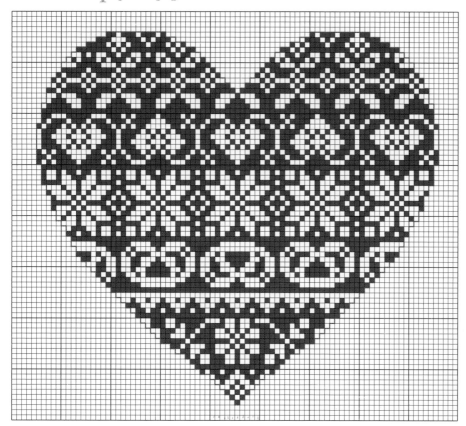

HEART WITH BIRDS (photo page 32)

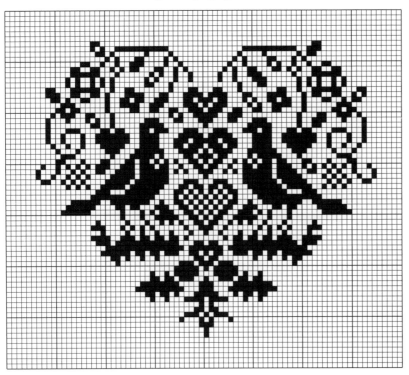

HEART WITH FOX (photo page 33)

791
792
3839

0123456789

BiENVENUE

2010

Feel free to change the look of this sampler by
embroidering it in blue, for example.

Feel free to change the look of this sampler by embroidering it in blue, for example.

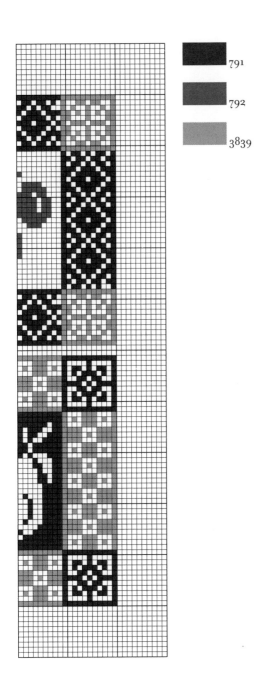

791

792

3839

SQUARE SAMPLER (photo page 50)

ABCDEFGHIJ
KLMNOPQRS
TUVWXYZ

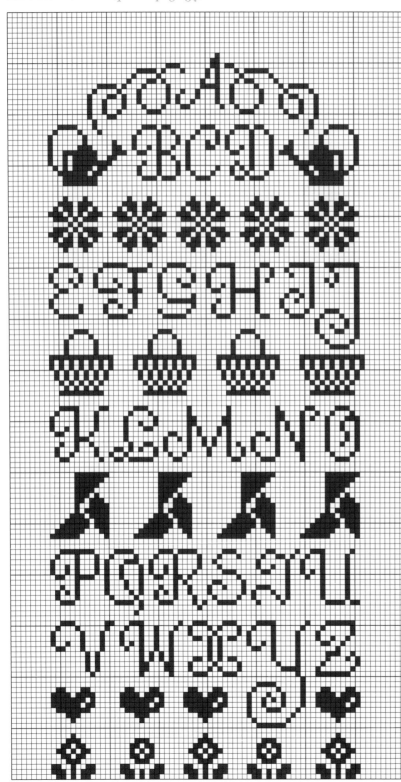

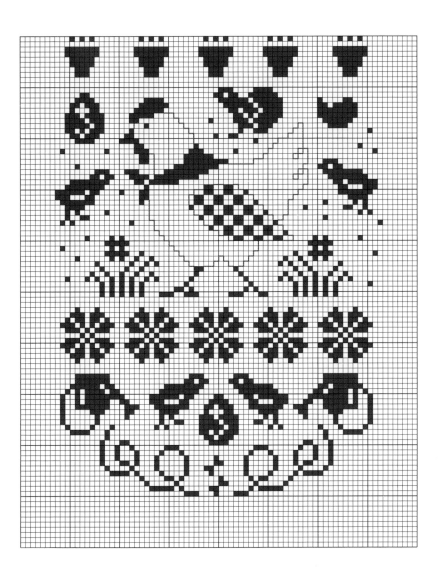

A chaque Jour Suffit Sa Peine

abcdefghijklmnopq
stuvwxyz

Acknowledgements

To everyone who helped to create this book, as well as all of those who have followed my work over these last fifteen years and who have contributed so much to the success of Passé Composé.

May we continue together down the road of our shared passion.

Passé Composé
29 Rue Albert Ier de Belgique
62000 Arras
Tel.: 06 07 50 30 51
www.marjoriemassey.com

First published in France in 2010 by Marabout
This edition published in Australia in 2012 by Murdoch Books Pty Limited

Murdoch Books Australia
Pier 8/9, 23 Hickson Road
Millers Point NSW 2000
Phone: +61 (0)2 8220 2000
Fax: +61 (0)2 8220 2558
www.murdochbooks.com.au
info@murdochbooks.com.au

Murdoch Books UK Limited
Erico House, 6th Floor
93–99 Upper Richmond Road
Putney, London SW15 2TG
Phone: +44 (0) 20 8785 5995
Fax: +44 (0) 20 8785 5985
www.murdochbooks.co.uk
info@murdochbooks.co.uk

For Corporate Orders & Custom Publishing contact Noel Hammond,
National Business Development Manager Murdoch Books Australia

Translator: Melissa McMahon
Editor: Georgina Bitcon
Design: Frédéric Voisin
Cover design: Miriam Steenhauer
Project Editor: Kit Carstairs
Production: Joan Beal

Text, design and illustration © Marabout 2010

National Library of Australia Cataloguing-in-Publication entry
Massey, Marjorie.
Cross-stitch samplers
ISBN 9781742661292 (hbk.)
Series: Made in France
Includes index.
Subjects: Cross-stitch.
Samplers. Embroidery. Cross-stitch--Patterns. Embroidery--Patterns.
746.433

A catalogue record for this book is available from the British Library.

Printed by 1010 Printing International Limited, China